The Unsolved Mystery of Bigfoot

Contents

1 A giant hairy mystery	2
2 Ancient tales of Bigfoot	4
3 **Theory 1:** Bigfoot is some kind of evolutionary leftover	6
4 Bigfoot, head to toe	10
5 The Yeti: Bigfoot's cold-climate cousin	12
6 Hairy creatures worldwide	14
7 **Theory 2:** Bigfoot sightings are just other animals	16
8 The business of Bigfoot	20
9 Bigfoot on film	22
10 **Theory 3:** Bigfoot is a hairy hoax	24
11 A conclusion? Or an ongoing mystery?	28
Glossary	29
Does Bigfoot exist?	30

Written by Mike Rampton

Collins

1 A giant hairy mystery

North America's enormous forests contain a mystery. Over the last hundred years, more than 3,000 people have reported seeing a bizarre creature there – a huge, hairy beast walking on two legs like a human, but bigger and more like an animal. Nobody knows what it is, or if it really exists.

All that tends to be found are enormous footprints. These have led to the creature's nickname: Bigfoot.

It's an interesting thought, that this giant, baffling monster might have been living in these forests for centuries. Despite there being no absolute evidence for Bigfoot's existence, or maybe *because* of this, the idea has really stuck around. But is there any truth to it?

2 Ancient tales of Bigfoot

One argument for Bigfoot's existence comes from ancient art. Painted Rock in California has thousand-year-old rock carvings that appear to show a family of large, hairy Bigfoot-like creatures.

The Cherokee people have ancient stories of giants, and the people known as Haudenosaunee tell stories of a hairy "stone giant" with thick, hard skin. Sasquatch (another name for Bigfoot) comes from a word in the Halq'eméylem language spoken in Canada: *Sasq'ets*, meaning "hairy man".

Pronunciation guide

Haudenosaune: hoh-den-uh-show-nee

Halq'eméylem: halk-uh-MAY-lum

Sasq'ets: ses-KEKs

A lot of similar stories seem to have arisen in groups of people that weren't in touch with one another. Is it just coincidence, or are the stories rooted in reality? Let's explore some theories.

3 Theory 1

Bigfoot is some kind of evolutionary leftover

Humans are part of a family of creatures called **hominids**, along with orangutans, chimpanzees and gorillas. Some people believe Bigfoot might be another, undiscovered hominid species, or an older species thought to be extinct.

Different scientists have suggested that Bigfoot might be various extinct hominids – *Gigantopithecus* or *Paranthropus* fit the bill.

Paranthropus

Gigantopithecus

However, *Gigantopithecus* lived in Asia, and *Paranthropus* in Africa. No fossils of either have been found in North America, home of Bigfoot sightings. For a population to have survived, they'd have to be living in fairly large groups – it seems unlikely that there would be no evidence of thousands of them living and dying over the centuries.

An expression sometimes used about Bigfoot is "missing link", the idea that, because humans **evolved** from apes, one day we'll discover a species halfway between apes and humans.

However, evolution is more complex than that – the changes that happen in a species to ensure it survives don't happen one after the other. Various changes happen at different times – some are useful and help the species go on and keep gradually evolving, while others don't.

It's much messier than a straight line, which means the idea of a missing link doesn't really make sense. More useful is the idea of a **last common ancestor**.

The last common ancestor of all existing hominids lived about 14 million years ago, meaning that if Bigfoot is indeed an ancient evolutionary leftover, they've done an amazing – some would say unlikely – job of staying hidden.

4 Bigfoot, head to toe

Over the years, reported Bigfoot sightings have been very different, so there isn't one clear picture of what it looks like.

Smell
One Bigfoot **eyewitness** described a smell "like a skunk that had rolled around in dead animals and hung around garbage". Lovely!

Feet
Footprints claimed to be Bigfoot's have measured up to 60 centimetres – over twice as long as most adult human's feet.

Face
Some sightings have described its face as very human-looking, while others have reported glowing eyes and sharp teeth.

Size
Reports vary, giving Bigfoot's height as anything from 1.8 metres to over four metres.

Hair
Bigfoot's hair or fur has been described as reddish brown, black or grey.

5 The Yeti: Bigfoot's cold-climate cousin

Beyond Bigfoot, the world's best-known mysterious hairy monster is the Yeti. There have been stories of Yeti sightings in the Himalayan mountains in Asia for hundreds of years, but they increased dramatically in the 19th and 20th centuries when mountaineering became popular and climbers reached higher heights. Mountaineers brought back photos of huge footprints, seemingly made by a **bipedal** creature …

The Yeti is said to be brown, grey or white, and up to 4.5 metres tall. It's also known as the Abominable Snowman. This is a poor translation from its name in Tibetan (the language spoken in the Himalayas), *metoh-kangmi*, which means "wild bear snowman", but "abominable" is fun to say.

Huge areas of the Himalayas are difficult to get to, so they remain unexplored. Are mysterious creatures hiding there?

13

6 Hairy creatures worldwide

There are stories of Bigfoot-like creatures everywhere. It's a world of hairy monsters!

Am Fear Liath Mòr (Scottish Highlands)

Also known as the Big Grey Man of Ben Macdui, this three-metre-tall creature terrifies mountaineers.

Orang Mawas (Johor, Malaysia)

The jungle-dwelling, vaguely fishy Orang Mawas stands three metres tall.

Barmanou (Northern Pakistan)

Terrified shepherds claim to have seen the Barmanou, a giant in animal fur making inhuman noises.

Yeren (Hubei, China)

The hairy, long-limbed, bulging-eyed, mountain-dwelling Yeren is said to laugh when it sees humans.

Yowie (Australia)

Aboriginal stories describe the Yowie as up to 3.6 metres tall, with long white hair and backwards feet.

7 Theory 2

Bigfoot sightings are just other animals

In an area known for Bigfoot sightings, you might think anything large that you can't identify must be Bigfoot, but there are other animals with similar traits.

The American black bear usually walks on all fours, but occasionally stands upright, and is over two metres tall when it does. There are more Bigfoot sightings in areas that have black bears than areas that don't, which supports that theory.

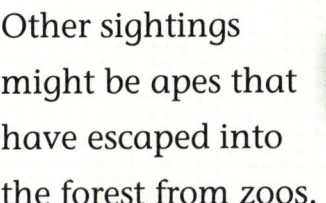

Other sightings might be apes that have escaped into the forest from zoos.

Sometimes people live in the wilderness and dress in furs.
They might seem quite Bigfoot-like.
People have been shot at in the woods by hunters who mistook them for Bigfoot, while reported sightings in North Carolina in 2017 turned out to be a man in a head-to-toe fur suit.

As for the Yeti, there are three species of bear in the Himalayas, all of which sometimes rear up: the Himalayan brown bear, Asiatic black bear and Tibetan blue bear. Bears walk on all fours, leaving different footprints to bipedal animals, but the Asiatic black bear sometimes puts its back legs into the prints from its front legs (like cats do), making it look like one giant footprint.

Asiatic black bear

Mountains are often misty, and mountaineering is tiring. Tired people are more likely to mistake one thing for another, and an unusual weather **phenomenon** called the "Brocken spectre" encourages this: the sun can cast shadows onto fog, so people sometimes see huge mysterious distant figures which are actually their own shadows. Spooky, but not monstrous!

shadow on the fog

8 The business of Bigfoot

More people have Bigfoot-related jobs than you might expect, given nobody knows if it even exists.

Mysteries are a great way to get people to visit places and spend money. There are Bigfoot museums all over the United States (with gift shops selling things like giant slippers), and Bigfoot tours where adventurers pay to be taken into the wilderness to see what they can spot.

There are "Bigfoot experts" who write books and give talks explaining their belief that Bigfoot is definitely real, and other experts who write books and give talks about how it definitely isn't.

If we ever discover the truth, a lot of people will find themselves with nothing to do!

9 Bigfoot on film

In 1967, two friends, Roger Patterson and Bob Gimlin, filmed what they said was a Bigfoot in the Californian forest. The footage is shaky, but their video has been watched millions of times.

Some experts say it just shows a man in a costume, but others insist the costume is too realistic for them to have made.

Cameras in 1967 weren't as good as they are now. This has added extra mysteries – for example, it's impossible to determine the speed the creature moves. Some of the creature's biological details are unlike any known apes, including its bottom!

We might never know the whole truth about that day, but whatever is shown in the video has become arguably the most famous image of Bigfoot.

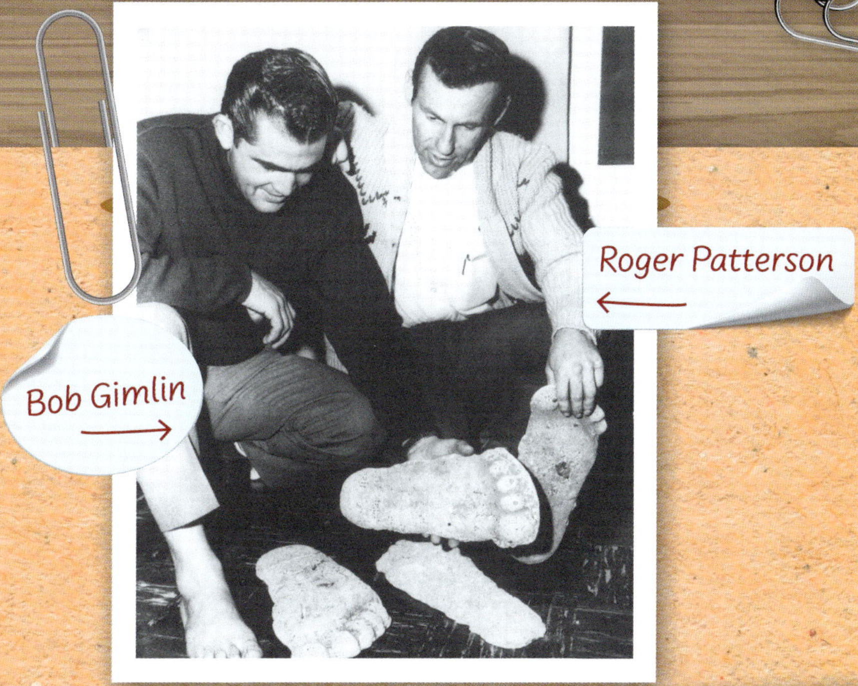

Bob Gimlin →

Roger Patterson ←

23

10 Theory 3

Bigfoot is a hairy hoax

Most scientists believe that most Bigfoot sightings are hoaxes – lies, tricks and fakery, made up for money, fame, attention or just fun. Most reported encounters are eyewitness accounts, which don't offer investigators much to investigate.

With footprints, dozens of plaster casts have been made over the years, which vary so much that there's no way they've come from one species. They have different structures and numbers of toes.

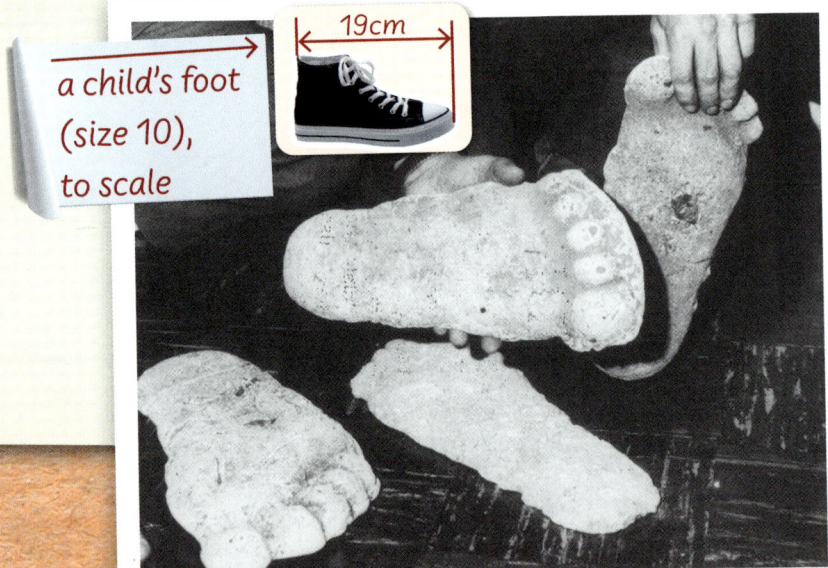

a child's foot (size 10), to scale

19cm

A "Bigfoot blood" sample presented to scientists was liquid that had leaked from a car. A clump of "Bigfoot fur" was hard to identify for a long time, until the realisation that it was actually … part of a wig!

One encounter, 1924's "Ape Canyon Incident", really spread the idea of Bigfoot. Newspapers described a "hairy man" with "sloping brows" who bullets bounced off. Unfortunately, it's thought to have been completely made up – decades later, some of the people involved even admitted to pressing fake footprints into the ground.

Something difficult both for hoaxers and Bigfoot investigators is the lack of any genuine scientific evidence: there's no agreed-upon description of any element of Bigfoot.

If you were lying about a bear, you'd learn about bears to make up a convincing story. With Bigfoot, there's so much inconsistent information out there, people create fake versions of a fake version of a fake version …

Sunday July 13th, 1924

IG APES REPORTED BY MINERS

11 A conclusion? Or an ongoing mystery?

The more we look into it, the more unlikely Bigfoot seems.

Most Bigfoot encounters surely come down to mistakes – thinking another animal is Bigfoot – or lies. Science doesn't support the idea that a large species could have been living under our noses this whole time barely detected.

However, while nobody can prove Bigfoot exists, we also can't prove that it doesn't. It *probably* doesn't, but it's such a fun mystery that it's hard not to want this enormous, bizarre creature to exist – it's awesome.

One day, an actual Bigfoot might be discovered. Until then, we can only conclude that it almost certainly doesn't exist.

Or does it …?

Glossary

bipedal two-legged, like the way humans walk

evolved changed and developed

eyewitness an account of events that someone saw with their own eyes

hominids members of the family of two-legged primates, living and extinct

last common ancestor the most recent creature from which a group of creatures is descended

phenomenon an unusual occurrence that is tricky to explain

Does Bigfoot exist?

Theory 1: Bigfoot is some kind of evolutionary leftover

It's a nice idea ... but evolution doesn't work like that!

chimpanzee

Gigantopithecus

Theory 2: Bigfoot sightings are just other animals

Everywhere Bigfoot has been seen, there are animals that fit the bill!

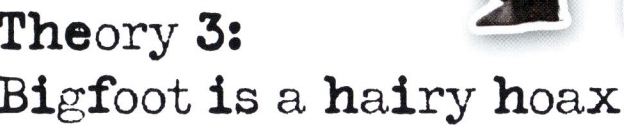

Theory 3: Bigfoot is a hairy hoax

There have definitely been a lot of hoaxes, but is every sighting a lie?

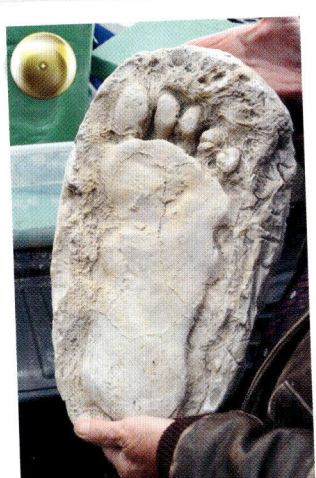

We may never know!

 Ideas for reading

Written by Gill Matthews
Primary Literacy Consultant

Reading objectives:
- be introduced to non-fiction books that are structured in different ways
- draw on what they already know or on background information and vocabulary provided by the teacher
- check that the text makes sense to them as they read and correct inaccurate reading
- answer and ask questions

Spoken language objectives:
- ask relevant questions to extend their understanding and knowledge
- use relevant strategies to build their vocabulary
- articulate and justify answers, arguments and opinions

Curriculum links: Science: animals, including humans

Interest words: enormous, bizarre, baffling, absolute

Build a context for reading

- Ask children to look at the front cover and to read the title. Discuss what they think the picture shows.
- Read the back-cover blurb. Ask what they think Bigfoot might be.
- Point out that this is an information text. Ask what they know about non-fiction books. Discuss the typical features of non-fiction.
- Ask children to find the contents page. Discuss the purpose and organisation of a contents.
- Ask children to use the contents to find Chapter 1.

Understand and apply reading strategies

- Read pp2–5 aloud, asking the children to follow in their books. Ask them what evidence they have found that makes them think Bigfoot does, or doesn't exist. Encourage them to support their responses with references to the text.
- Ask children to read pp6–9. Ask what they think about this theory. Encourage them to support their responses with opinions and evidence.